Francis Frith's
North Buckinghamshire

MARTIN ANDREW is an architectural and landscape historian, and a writer on outdoor matters; he is the Conservation Officer for Wycombe District Council in Buckinghamshire. He specialises in the landscape of lowland England, and combines his love of history, landscape and architecture in his writing. Since 1978 he has lived in Haddenham in Buckinghamshire with his wife and children. He is a keen long-distance walker and enjoys riding his classic motor cycle round the country lanes of the Chilterns. He was born in Doncaster, but spent most of his childhood in Ealing and Carshalton in Surrey. After university he worked for the Greater London Council's Historic Buildings Division, Buckinghamshire County Council and Salisbury District Council, before joining Wycombe District Council in 1990.

Photographic Memories

Francis Frith's
North
Buckinghamshire

Martin Andrew

First published in the United Kingdom in 2002 by
Frith Book Company Ltd

Hardback Edition 2002
ISBN 1-85937-626-6

British Library Cataloguing in Publication Data

Francis Frith's North Buckinghamshire
Martin Andrew

Frith Book Company Ltd
Frith's Barn, Teffont,
Salisbury, Wiltshire SP3 5QP
Tel: +44 (0) 1722 716 376
Email: info@francisfrith.co.uk
www.francisfrith.co.uk

Printed and bound in Great Britain

Front Cover: Aylesbury, Market Square 1901 47462

Contents

Francis Frith: *Victorian Pioneer*

FRANCIS FRITH, Victorian founder of the world-famous photographic archive, was a complex and multi-talented man. A devout Quaker and a highly successful Victorian businessman, he was both philosophic by nature and pioneering in outlook.

By 1855 Francis Frith had already established a wholesale grocery business in Liverpool, and sold it for the astonishing sum of £200,000, which is the equivalent today of over £15,000,000. Now a multi-millionaire, he was able to indulge his passion for travel. As a child he had pored over travel books written by early explorers, and his fancy and imagination had been stirred by family holidays to the sublime mountain regions of Wales and Scotland. 'What a land of spirit-stirring and enriching scenes and places!' he had written. He was to return to these scenes of grandeur in later years to 'recapture the thousands of vivid and tender memories', but with a different purpose. Now in his thirties, and captivated by the new science of photography, Frith set out on a series of pioneering journeys to the Nile regions that occupied him from 1856 until 1860.

Intrigue and Adventure

He took with him on his travels a specially-designed wicker carriage that acted as both dark-room and sleeping chamber. These far-flung journeys were packed with intrigue and adventure. In his life story, written when he was sixty-three, Frith tells of being held captive by bandits, and of fighting 'an awful midnight battle to the very point of surrender with a deadly pack of hungry, wild dogs'. Sporting flowing Arab costume, Frith arrived at Akaba by camel seventy years before Lawrence, where he encountered 'desert princes and rival sheikhs, blazing with jewel-hilted swords'.

During these extraordinary adventures he was assiduously exploring the desert regions bordering the Nile and patiently recording the antiquities and peoples with his camera. He was the first photographer to venture beyond the sixth cataract. Africa was still the mysterious 'Dark Continent', and Stanley and Livingstone's historic meeting was a decade into the future. The conditions for picture taking confound belief. He laboured for hours in his wicker dark-room in the sweltering heat of the desert, while the volatile chemicals fizzed dangerously in their trays. Often he was forced to work in remote tombs and caves where conditions were cooler. Back in London he exhibited his photographs and was 'rapturously cheered' by members of the Royal Society. His reputation as a

photographer was made overnight. An eminent modern historian has likened their impact on the population of the time to that on our own generation of the first photographs taken on the surface of the moon.

Venture of a Life-Time

Characteristically, Frith quickly spotted the opportunity to create a new business as a specialist publisher of photographs. He lived in an era of immense and sometimes violent change. For the poor in the early part of Victoria's reign work was a drudge and the hours long, and people had precious little free time to enjoy themselves. Most had no transport other than a cart or gig at their disposal, and had not travelled far beyond the boundaries of their own town or village. However,

by the 1870s, the railways had threaded their way across the country, and Bank Holidays and half-day Saturdays had been made obligatory by Act of Parliament. All of a sudden the ordinary working man and his family were able to enjoy days out and see a little more of the world.

With characteristic business acumen, Francis Frith foresaw that these new tourists would enjoy having souvenirs to commemorate their days out. In 1860 he married Mary Ann Rosling and set out with the intention of photographing every city, town and village in Britain. For the next thirty years he travelled the country by train and by pony and trap, producing fine photographs of seaside resorts and beauty spots that were keenly bought by millions of Victorians. These prints were painstakingly pasted into family albums and pored over during the dark nights of winter, rekindling precious memories of summer excursions.

The Rise of Frith & Co

Frith's studio was soon supplying retail shops all over the country. To meet the demand he gathered about him a small team of photographers, and published the work of independent artist-photographers of the calibre of Roger Fenton and Francis Bedford. In order to gain some understanding of the scale of Frith's business one only has to look at the catalogue issued by Frith & Co in 1886: it runs to some 670 pages, listing not only many thousands of views of the British Isles but also many photographs of most European countries, and China, Japan, the USA and Canada – note the sample page shown above from the hand-written *Frith & Co* ledgers detailing pictures taken. By 1890 Frith had created the greatest specialist photographic publishing company in the world,

Frith's death, a new card measuring 5.5 x 3.5 inches became the standard format, but it was not until 1902 that the divided back came into being, with address and message on one face and a full-size illustration on the other. *Frith & Co* were in the vanguard of postcard development, and Frith's sons Eustace and Cyril continued their father's monumental task, expanding the number of views offered to the public and recording more and more places in Britain, as the coasts and countryside were opened up to mass travel.

Francis Frith died in 1898 at his villa in Cannes, his great project still growing. The archive he created continued in business for another seventy years. By 1970 it contained over a third of a million pictures of 7,000 cities, towns and villages. The massive photographic record Frith has left to us stands as a living monument to a special and very remarkable man.

with over 2,000 outlets – more than the combined number that Boots and WH Smith have today! The picture on the right shows the *Frith & Co* display board at Ingleton in the Yorkshire Dales. Beautifully constructed with mahogany frame and gilt inserts, it could display up to a dozen local scenes.

Postcard Bonanza

The ever-popular holiday postcard we know today took many years to develop. In 1870 the Post Office issued the first plain cards, with a pre-printed stamp on one face. In 1894 they allowed other publishers' cards to be sent through the mail with an attached adhesive halfpenny stamp. Demand grew rapidly, and in 1895 a new size of postcard was permitted called the court card, but there was little room for illustration. In 1899, a year after

Frith's Archive: *A Unique Legacy*

FRANCIS FRITH'S legacy to us today is of immense significance and value, for the magnificent archive of evocative photographs he created provides a unique record of change in 7,000 cities, towns and villages throughout Britain over a century and more. Frith and his fellow studio photographers revisited locations many times down the years to update their views, compiling for us an enthralling and colourful pageant of British life and character.

We tend to think of Frith's sepia views of Britain as nostalgic, for most of us use them to conjure up memories of places in our own lives with which we have family associations. It often makes us forget that to Francis Frith they were records of daily life as it was actually being lived in the cities, towns and villages of his day. The Victorian age was one of great and often bewildering change for ordinary people, and though the pictures evoke an impression of slower times, life was as busy and hectic as it is today.

We are fortunate that Frith was a photographer of the people, dedicated to recording the minutiae of everyday life. For it is this sheer wealth of visual data, the painstaking chronicle of changes in dress, transport, street layouts, buildings, housing, engineering and landscape that captivates us so much today. His remarkable images offer us a powerful link with the past and with the lives of our ancestors.

Today's Technology

Computers have now made it possible for Frith's many thousands of images to be accessed almost instantly. In the Frith archive today, each photograph is carefully 'digitised' then stored on a CD Rom. Frith archivists can locate a single photograph amongst thousands within seconds. Views can be catalogued and sorted under a variety of categories of place and content to the immediate benefit of researchers.

Inexpensive reference prints can be created for them at the touch of a mouse button, and a wide range of books and other printed materials assembled and published for a wider, more general readership - in the next twelve months over a hundred Frith local history titles will be published! The day-to-day workings of the archive are very different from how they were in Francis Frith's time: imagine the herculean task of sorting through eleven tons of glass negatives as Frith had to do to locate a particular sequence of pictures! Yet

See Frith at www.francisfrith.co.uk

the archive still prides itself on maintaining the same high standards of excellence laid down by Francis Frith, including the painstaking cataloguing and indexing of every view.

It is curious to reflect on how the internet now allows researchers in America and elsewhere greater instant access to the archive than Frith himself ever enjoyed. Many thousands of individual views can be called up on screen within seconds on one of the Frith internet sites, enabling people living continents away to revisit the streets of their ancestral home town, or view places in Britain where they have enjoyed holidays. Many overseas researchers welcome the chance to view special theme selections, such as transport, sports, costume and ancient monuments.

We are certain that Francis Frith would have heartily approved of these modern developments in imaging techniques, for he himself was always working at the very limits of Victorian photographic technology.

The Value of the Archive Today

Because of the benefits brought by the computer, Frith's images are increasingly studied by social historians, by researchers into genealogy and ancestory, by architects, town planners, and by teachers and schoolchildren involved in local history projects.

In addition, the archive offers every one of us an opportunity to examine the places where we and our families have lived and worked down the years. Highly successful in Frith's own era, the archive is now, a century and more on, entering a new phase of popularity.

The Past in Tune with the Future

Historians consider the Francis Frith Collection to be of prime national importance. It is the only archive of its kind remaining in private ownership and has been valued at a million pounds. However, this figure is now rapidly increasing as digital technology enables more and more people around the world to enjoy its benefits.

Francis Frith's archive is now housed in an historic timber barn in the beautiful village of Teffont in Wiltshire. Its founder would not recognize the archive office as it is today. In place of the many thousands of dusty boxes containing glass plate negatives and an all-pervading odour of photographic chemicals, there are now ranks of computer screens. He would be amazed to watch his images travelling round the world at unimaginable speeds through network and internet lines.

The archive's future is both bright and exciting. Francis Frith, with his unshakeable belief in making photographs available to the greatest number of people, would undoubtedly approve of what is being done today with his lifetime's work. His photographs, depicting our shared past, are now bringing pleasure and enlightenment to millions around the world a century and more after his death.

North Buckinghamshire
An Introduction

BUCKINGHAMSHIRE is a county that falls easily into two parts, with the chalk Chiltern Hills defining the north edge of the southern parts. As soon as we drop off the Chiltern scarp, we are in the Midlands, where the open field farming of the Middle Ages dominates all the way from Wendover to the Northamptonshire border. This landscape is radically different from the south, with its chalk hills clad in beech woods with narrow winding high-hedged lanes linking small hamlets, and in places large hedgeless arable fields. In the south there are some fine market towns, and several sparkling chalk rivers and winterbournes; but it is an inward-looking landscape. Nevertheless, there are fine views from the chalk ridge northwards over the Vale of Aylesbury.

Northern Buckinghamshire, however, is completely different. There is relatively little woodland, and the villages are larger and more nucleated and set within their large hedged fields. Virtually all had the Midland medieval two-, three-, or four-field crop rotation system of farming, with strips apportioned among the villagers and one of the fields lying fallow each year. There were very few farmhouses outside the villages, which in many cases never entirely coalesced; so many Bucks villages have a number of 'ends', or clusters and groupings of houses and cottages. Haddenham, for example, has three 'ends' linked by scattered cottages; Sherington also has three 'ends', each one focussed on the parish church.

This open-field farming continued well into the 19th century, but the enclosure movement, whereby bigger landholders grouped together to divide the open fields up into regular fenced and hedged fields, got under way in the 18th century. Enclosure transformed the county into its present appearance of villages with older houses, and farmsteads out in the fields built after the enclosure award. For example, Haddenham which, like nearby Long Crendon, held out until well into the 19th century with an Enclosure Act passed in 1830, has several farmsteads out towards the parish boundary which were built in the mid 1830s. This story could be repeated for most north Bucks villages. In many areas the enclosure hedges cut across the evidence of the medieval farming system, where ridge-and-furrow survives in many pasture fields. Ridge-and-furrow looks as if the field has been covered in giant corrugations, often curving in an S-shape to reflect the turning motion of an ancient plough team: there are thousands of acres of ridge-and-furrow surviving in the county north of the Chiltern Hills.

In north Bucks ranges of hills run diagonally across the county from south-west to north-east, and these produce building stone. A belt across the middle to the north of Aylesbury produces a crumbly Portland limestone, seen in Whitchurch and Oving, while south of the Northamptonshire border a harder oolitic limestone gives villages like Hanslope and Lavendon their character. In the far east, around the Brickhills and outcropping elsewhere, at Brill for instance, the Lower Greensand produced a toffee-coloured sandstone; while around Haddenham there is a tradition of earth wall or cob building, locally known as witchert (white earth). Apart from the stone and cob, timber-framing and brick are the main building materials, with tiles, thatch and slate for roofs. Among the innumerable attractive villages are a number of fine market towns, none too large (although some have greatly expanded since the 1960s, when this book finishes), such as Aylesbury and Buckingham.

Other towns of quality include Winslow, Newport Pagnell, Wendover and Stony Stratford. From the late 1960s the new city of Milton Keynes swallowed up huge tracts of farmland in the central north-east of the county; but it does not feature in this book, as the latest views were taken in around 1965.

The rolling countryside is most attractive, and there are very few flat and uninteresting areas, even in the Vale of Aylesbury and the Buckingham clay vales. Numerous streams feed a number of rivers, the Thame in the south and the Ouzel and the Great Ouse to the north. There is also an artificial waterway that threads through the county from Marsworth east of Aylesbury to leave it near Wolverton in the north: the Grand Junction Canal, built between 1793 and 1805. It became the Grand Union Canal by merger with others in 1929, and had two branch canals in Buckinghamshire: the Wendover Arm opened in 1797, and the Aylesbury Arm opened in 1815. The canal tow paths add immeasurably to the footpath network of Buckinghamshire north of the Chiltern Hills. The North Bucks Way long-distance footpath developed by the Ramblers Association is a wonderful route through the area covered in this book, running as it does from the Chilterns right through the county to Wolverton. For riders there is the Swan's Way, which also bisects the county from south to north.

I have lived in Haddenham at the south end of the area covered in this book since 1978, and have walked many hundreds of miles of its footpaths,

visiting all of its villages and towns many times. I have a considerable affection for the county. To many, Buckinghamshire is a county to drive through on their way elsewhere, perhaps along the M1 motorway or along the ancient Roman routes of Watling Street (the A5) or Akeman Street (the A41). To others, the county is the new city of Milton Keynes, the unjustified butt of jokes and ill-informed sneers. Visit it to judge for yourself: few modern towns can boast as many trees or as much greenery and linear parks. It is not all concrete cows.

Buckinghamshire is an ancient county: it was certainly in existence as an administrative unit in 1016. However, about a century before this, during the Anglo-Danish wars, when Edward the Elder, King of Wessex, began his re-conquest of the area ceded to the victorious Danes, the Anglo-Saxon Chronicle records under the year 917 AD: 'In the same year before Martinmas (11 November) King Edward went to Buckingham with his levies and was there for four weeks, constructing both of the fortifications, one on each side of the river, before he left'. Apart from referring to Buckingham by name, this also shows that there was already a town which it was necessary to fortify. The English counties grew up to provide the territorial base for the defence of what became the county towns such

as Buckingham. The idea was that each 'hide' should provide a soldier for the town's defences. Thus the county's dimensions were created - although it seems likely that the Chilterns area was added later in the 10th century.

The odd consequence of all this is that the county town was in the north-west corner of a county about 50 miles long, and wasp-waisted around Aylesbury. In the Middle Ages it remained a county somewhat on the periphery. There were no major monasteries to rival St Albans Abbey in neighbouring Hertfordshire: it was a county of small religious houses, such as Lavendon Abbey, Notley Abbey near Long Crendon or Tickford Priory in Newport Pagnell. There are few monastic remains, and most of the parish churches are relatively small - the exceptions include Newport Pagnell and Olney. The towns were small too, and remained so until well into the 19th century. Many market towns were established in the Middle Ages, ranging from the larger ones like Aylesbury, Newport Pagnell, Stony Stratford and Wendover to smaller ones such as Olney and Winslow; others are now no more than villages, such as Hanslope and Whitchurch.

In the 18th century, many of the timber-framed towns and villages used their increased agricultural and trading wealth to rebuild or re-front in brick or stone, and the predominantly Georgian and early-

19th century character and appearance of the historic towns emerged. A remarkable amount of pre-1850 architecture survives in the county north of the Chilterns. A stroll round Buckingham, Wendover, Winslow, Stony Stratford, Newport Pagnell and even parts of Aylesbury is very rewarding architecturally: fine Georgian fronts often conceal timber-framed houses, while stone-built medieval parish churches enrich virtually every town and village. Within villages, there is perhaps more variety: numerous timber-framed and thatched cottages from the 16th and 17th centuries remain little changed, while brick and stone houses and cottages were added. Many villages are 'chocolate box' ones, such as Oving, Long Crendon or Calverton, while others are more workaday, partly because the Victorian and 20th-century additions are less sympathetic. Several of the villages in this book fall into this category, and Frith's photographers do not spare their blushes: Sherington, Grendon Underwood, Steeple Claydon and Woburn Sands are good examples.

North Buckinghamshire was never industrialised, apart from breweries and the like, but the 19th century saw new industry and ways of earning a living arrive. This is most conspicuous with the arrival of the railways in the 1830s, for Wolverton was selected as the London and Birmingham Railway's halfway house, being roughly equidistant between the two cities. New Wolverton really developed after the merger in 1846 that produced the London and North Western Railway, and the town grew to accommodate the workforce building locomotives and railway carriages. The town was laid out in a rectangular grid of streets, like the other nearby railway village of New Bradwell in the 1850s.

Elsewhere industrial growth was more sporadic: for example, the brick industry around Bletchley,

the condensed milk factory (now Nestlé's) and Hazell Watson and Viney's printing works (now demolished) in Aylesbury, or Wipac in Buckingham. The biggest change in the 20th century, for the relatively sleepy and contented northern part of the county, was undoubtedly the arrival of Milton Keynes from 1967 onwards. Aylesbury, Buckingham and Bletchley expanded greatly. Aylesbury grew most, being the county town, a role which it had begun to take on during the later Middle Ages and which was complete by the 17th century, a fact which deeply annoyed the citizens of Buckingham. Championed by the influential Earls Temple and Dukes of Buckingham at nearby Stowe, Buckingham regained the Summer Assizes for about fifty years either side of 1800, but it was a temporary reprieve; Aylesbury is very much the county town nowadays.

At the end of the period covered in these Frith views, the section of the M1 through Buckinghamshire opened in 1959: there are two views of it near Newport Pagnell with very few vehicles on it, which demonstrate how much traffic has increased in the intervening forty years. However, the county north of the Chiltern Hills retains its historic character, and is under-rated by those who rush through to points west and north. I consider Buckinghamshire the equal of most in the English lowlands, and I hope this collection of views illustrates this. It is a county with history at every turn. It is rich in historic architecture, with country houses in landscaped parks (Stowe is of European importance, for example, and who could forget Waddeson Manor on its hill top?), in fine villages and in landscape history. I hope you enjoy this selection of views, some from the late 19th century but most from the 1950s and 1960s - the latter decades with relatively little-changed architecture and views, but adorned with antiquated motor cars that belong to another age.

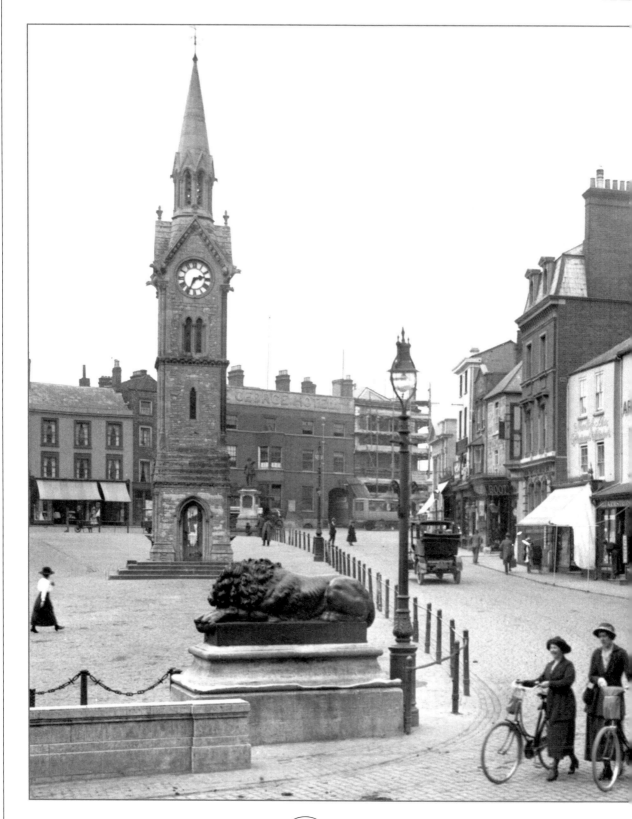

Aylesbury and the South

Aylesbury, Market Square 1921 70553
The first chapter starts, appropriately enough, in the county town of Aylesbury. From the late Middle Ages onwards, Aylesbury gradually supplanted Buckingham after which the county is named (see Chapter 3); by the 17th century, the circuit judges heard county cases only in Aylesbury. The centre of the town is Market Square, whose origins are medieval although the town only got a royal charter in 1553. The photographer is looking across from County Hall.

▼ **Aylesbury, County Hall 1897** 39626
The south side of the Market Square is dominated by the very fine Georgian County Hall built for the county assizes. It was a long time a-building, taking from 1722 until 1737. The central arched window had a balcony outside, which was the public scaffold from which criminals were hanged - the last public execution was in 1845. After a disastrous fire in 1970 the interior of the courts were lovingly recreated, accurate in every detail down to the crested chamber pot behind the judge's seat. At the left is the Jacobean-style Corn Exchange of 1865.

▼ **Aylesbury, Market Square 1921** 70551
Here we see a livestock sale in the Market Square, the sheep penned and the cattle tied to improvised rails. The last livestock market in the square took place a few years later, in 1927. The Midland Bank on the left was brand new in 1921. All to its right, including one of the two small white buildings, has since been replaced by rather poor 1960s buildings. At the left is the 1911 statue of John Hampden, the great Parliamentary leader of the 1630s and the English Civil War. It was moved 50 feet east in 1988.

◄ **Aylesbury, Market Square 1901** 47462
A livestock sale is under way, with the auctioneer's tent behind the clock tower. On the left the pipe-smoker sits on his hurdle waggon waiting to collect the livestock pens after the sale has finished. The clock tower was erected in 1876 on the approximate site of the old market house, which was pulled down in 1866 to enlarge the market place. The lion drowsing on its plinth is one of a pair of French cast-iron statues, a gift from Ferdinand, Baron Rothschild of Waddesdon Manor in 1887.

◄ **Aylesbury, The Bell Hotel 1921** 70563
Next to County Hall is the Bell Hotel, which had been altered and improved in 1919. The plain stuccoed Regency frontage was embellished by brick piers and other brickwork, while the shallow-pitched slate roof was replaced by a dormered mansard to increase accommodation. The angled corner entrance is now a window. The creeper-clad house beyond the motor cars is now a Barclays Bank, but retains its domestic facade.

Aylesbury, Walton Street 1921 70558
Frith's photographer looks past the Bell Hotel down Walton Street - a scene now much changed. At the right the jewellers, the Greyhound on the east side of Market Square, and the buildings beyond on the right-hand side of Walton Street are part of what was demolished in the early 1960s for the Friars Square shopping centre and the new County Offices; the latter is a twelve-storey tower block, visible for miles around and much-hated, nicknamed 'Fred's Folly' after Fred Pooley, the then County Architect - it is in fact a rather refined building.

◀ **Aylesbury, Market Place c1955**
A84019
The war memorial (foreground) arrived in about 1920 after World War I. Further names of Aylesbury men who died for their country had to be added after World War II. The buildings on the left as far as the white building with the blind extended have been replaced, mostly in the 1960s. We may be thankful that the grandiose 1860s Italianate building beyond, once Boots and nowadays a Halifax branch, does survive.

◀ **Aylesbury, Kingsbury Square 1901**
47464
Probably the original market place, and nearer the parish church whose tower looms in the background, Kingsbury Square was laid out in the Middle Ages and has several good, old buildings including the 16th-century The Rookwood. The houses on the left, by 1901 shops but retaining front gardens, were replaced in the 1960s by mediocre offices over a shop. Beyond them, the tall building is the Victoria Working Men's Club, built in 1887 to commemorate Queen Victoria's Golden Jubilee and funded by the ubiquitous Baron Rothschild of Waddesdon.

▼ **Aylesbury, Market Square c1955** A84050
This view looks along the north side of Market Square past the war memorial into Cambridge Street on the left of the Round House and the High Street to its right. Burton's (left) in the company's typical Art Deco style was built in 1936, and replaced the George Inn. The Round House itself replaced an earlier stuccoed version. Beyond is the early 1960s five-storey office building that simultaneously ruins the streets either side of it.

◀ **Aylesbury, Cambridge Street c1955** A84028
Cambridge Street, misleadingly, does not head for Cambridge, and was formerly Bakers Lane. It is now a one-way street - the far end was demolished for the inner relief road. Ye Olde Harrow Inn back entrance has a bacon shop on the left. The pub has now merged with the Barleycorn on the Buckingham Street corner and is archly renamed the Farmyard and Firkin. More survives on the right, while the three-storey building on the left, dated 1897, also survives.

▼ **Aylesbury, High Street c1955** A84040
Now we head down High Street, until the later 19th century dominated by houses rather than commerce. Beyond the car is the north side of Market Square, with the Art Deco Burtons the first building visible. The gabled 1860s buildings on the left survive, but the hipped-roofed building beyond was rebuilt in the 1960s and 1980s. The National Provincial Bank is gone, and the shop beyond was replaced by a crass narrow five-storey early 1960s block that ruins views up the High Street.

▼ **Aylesbury, High Street c1955** A84056
Further down the High Street, we are looking past the junction with Britannia Street with John Collier (now a bathroom store) and Marks and Spencer's beyond in their neo-Georgian premises of 1938. These replaced Longley's the drapers, then with the most glazing of any shop in the town by far. The 1840s terrace in the foreground has been demolished, apart from the part to the right of the lamppost, partly in the 1960s and partly in the 1990s.

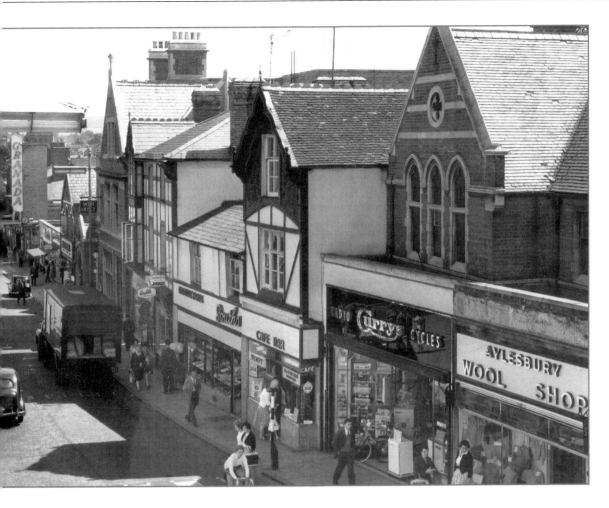

▲ **Aylesbury, High Street c1960**
A84057
We are near Marks and
Spencer's. The buildings on the
right up to the post office were
replaced by the Hale Leys
shopping centre in 1988. The
1890s post office, an
Elizabethan-style brick building
with stone dressings with an
elegant gable, fell victim to
modern ideas and was replaced
in the 1960s by a flat-roofed
box. The Granada cinema
beyond survives as Gala Bingo.
In the far distance is the now-
demolished Hazell, Watson and
Viney printing works with its tall
chimney.

◀ **Aylesbury, St Mary's
Square c1955** A84021
Behind Kingsbury is St
Mary's Square, in fact the
churchyard of the medieval
parish church and a green
oasis in the town. The
railings went during the
Second World War and
have never been replaced;
only the low wall and the
gates themselves escaped
and survive. This view looks
north past the 1840s Old
Parish School, now part of
the County Museum - the
second gable is a 1907
replica.

Aylesbury, Parsons Fee c1965 A84097
Parsons Fee leads uphill from Castle Street towards the church with timber-framed ranges and then St Osyths, a good brick house of about 1700, its facade now painted. Beyond it are the grounds of The Prebendal behind high brick walls. From 1757 to 1764 it was the home of John Wilkes, the radical MP for Aylesbury, and is now the offices of the publisher, Ginn and Co.

Aylesbury, The Vale Park c1950 A84007
At the bottom end of the High Street is The Vale, a park formally opened in 1937 in fields between the now vanished London and North Western Railway station (demolished in 1960) and the gas works, also now gone. Now a smart covered swimming pool replaces the old open air Vale Pool, but the park is relatively little changed. The drinking fountain was originally installed in 1914 in Kingsbury, but was moved here after 1929.

Aylesbury, The Canal and a Lock 1897 39643
First authorised in the 1790s, the Aylesbury Arm finally opened in 1815, running from the Grand Junction Canal at Marsworth across the Vale of Aylesbury. Coal was one of the main early imports, and local prices fell dramatically. This view looks towards the town past Lock No 16, near Hills and Partridges (their works now replaced by Tesco's), to the original brick canal bridge, rebuilt in 1900.

Aylesbury, The Milk Factory 1897 39640
The coal wharves at the canal basin by Walton Street were soon joined by factories along the canal. One that arrived in 1870 to take advantage both of the canal and the milk from the Vale of Aylesbury dairy herds was the Anglo-Swiss Condensed Milk Company, later Nestlé's factory, still functioning. Here the photographer looks across the canal from the meadow (now occupied by housing) to the factory, nowadays somewhat changed; it had great dignity with its range of gables and sash windows.

Aylesbury, The Canal 1897 39642
This view is from the towpath beside the Nestlé factory with boys fishing from a small wharf - it still survives. The bridge is the one in 39643 (page 27), rebuilt in 1900, and through the arch are the lock gates to Lock No 16. The meadow across the canal is now occupied by 1990s housing, Hilda Wharf.

▼ **Stoke Mandeville, The Hospital, The Driveway c1965** s569044

The world-famous Stoke Mandeville Hospital started life as the Aylesbury Isolation Hospital. This view shows the main buildings with their stripped-down, simplified Classicism popular in the 1930s. These survive; the portico is still the main entrance, although numerous other buildings went up during and after World War II. These include the Spinal Injuries Unit, finished in 1983, now an acknowledged centre of excellence.

▼ **Wendover, View from the South-West 1901** 44772

Wendover lies just off the Chiltern Hills at the head of a gap through the hills, a continuation north of the Misbourne valley. This view was taken from the foot of Bacombe Hill, where a track, now part of the Ridgeway Long Distance Path, leaves the Ellesborough Road to climb to Coombe Hill. The railway to Aylesbury, opened in 1891, crosses in the middle distance. The fields between the town and the wooded hills - Wendover Woods - are now partially covered in housing estates.

Wendover, View from the North-East 1901

44773

The field from which this view was taken is now a residential street named Honeybanks. This may be a reference to Banks Farm, whose barns can be seen beyond the hedge. The view looks past the clock tower and along the High Street. In the distance is Coombe Hill, which rises to 853 feet; a Boer War Memorial obelisk now stands on the summit, erected in 1904.

Wendover, The Clock Tower c1955 W51012
Situated at the junction of the High Street, Aylesbury Road and Tring Road, this was erected in 1842 as a market hall and lock-up by the then lord of the manor, Abel Smith. In 1870 a clock tower and belfry were added. It was converted to house a small fire engine, but nowadays it is a Tourist Information Centre. Beyond is a K1 1920s telephone box, now replaced by the familiar K6 type.

Wendover, Aylesbury Road c1965 W51033
Aylesbury Road is one of the town's best roads, with its wide grassed verge on the east side still lined with mature trees. Here are some of the best houses, many with dignified Georgian frontages hiding Tudor or 17th-century timber-framed structures. The Red House to the left of the tree is a case in point: its elegant brick facade with the original 1740s sashes and pedimented doorcase conceals a 17th-century timber frame. On the right The Old Cottage, No 9, still has exposed timber-framing.

Wendover, Aylesbury Road c1955 W51011
We are a little further north-west, and the clock tower disappears from view. The view is little changed since the 1950s, apart from more parked cars. Sturrick House on the far left, once a temperance hotel, is 16th-century, but the ground floor frontage is 18th-century. The building on the far right, Manor Farm House, has a rendered front concealing a jettied timber-framed house of about 1600.

◀ **Haddenham, Banks's Pond c1960** H375036
Haddenham is a very large village. The original core winds through from south to north, and is characterised by 'witchert' or earth-wall houses, many thatched; streams and ponds run all through the village. Banks's Pond lies beside the main east-west road. In it swim the successors to a former important local industry, the rearing of Aylesbury ducks, the reason why the ponds were so useful. In the mid 1960s housing estates and shopping parades arrived, so this rural scene is now more suburban.

Wendover, High Street c1965 W51021

The High Street was laid out as the market place in the early 13th century when Wendover became a borough, and a wide and spacious one it was, running from Pound Street to Aylesbury Street. However, the inevitable encroachment took place: stalls became permanent buildings, and the buildings between Back Lane and the High Street infilled much of the north side. This view looks from the junction with South Street and Pound Street (behind the photographer) to the beginning of the encroachments, the then National Provincial Bank building (centre).

Wendover, The Parish Church c1955 W51015

The parish church of St Mary was left high and dry about half a mile to the south as the settlement migrated to the new market in the 13th century. It thus feels more like a country church than a town one, with a large pond between it and the footpath to town. The scene is little changed, except the gates from the 1871 lychgate have gone. Behind is the Manor House, mostly rebuilt by George Devey in the 1870s, and now a school.

Long Crendon, High Street 1962 L471014

North-east of Haddenham, Long Crendon is one of the county's most attractive villages. Like Haddenham, its medieval open fields were not enclosed until 1827. This meant prosperity was more widely spread, and so many more older houses and cottages survived (there are still at least 30 medieval houses). This view looks east along the High Street past the turn to Wapping and gives a good idea of the range of houses - medieval, 17th-century and later - and of the mix of building materials - stone, timber-framing, brick, tile and thatch.

Oakley, The Parish Church 1952 065007

Further north-west along the Thame to Bicester road, the village of Oakley has suffered from very considerable rebuilding from the 1960s onwards. These views are therefore more of a record of the past than usual. The main road has been improved, so the wall and mighty oak tree on the left have gone; Churchfield House behind lost some of its grounds in the process. The post and rail fence to the right has been renewed and guards a stream, with Manor Farm beyond.

Oakley, The Parish Church c1960 065008

Oakley was within the medieval royal hunting forest of Bernwood - the king's hunting lodge cum palace was at Brill nearby. The name of the village means 'a clearing in the oak woods'. The forest lasted until 1632 when Charles I disafforested it to raise revenue, so Oakley's medieval parish church used to look out on a more wooded scene. The nave is mainly 12th-century, while the 14th-century south chapel has an external arched tomb recess under its three-light window (centre).

Oakley, Post Office Corner c1960 065001
This view looking towards the Bicester Road along The Turnpike has changed rather dramatically. The house on the left disappeared when the road was widened. The house to the right behind the signpost (also gone) is now the entrance to School Lane, a close of 1970s bungalows. The outbuilding on the right survives, although much renewed and incorporated into the Old Bakery; so does the part timber-framed 17th-century house with the unusual panelled central chimney stack.

Oakley, The Village c1960 065005
Again a much-changed view, this time looking into The Turnpike from Manor Road. The rather delightful cottage on the right behind its iron railings went in the 1960s to be replaced by humdrum modern houses. It takes a close examination of the present Chandos Arms to recognise that it is the same building as in this photograph. In 1960 it was still a small village alehouse.

▼ **Grendon Underwood, Crucks c1960** G230005
The name of this cottage is a reminder of a very important medieval and late
medieval building tradition in this area, possibly associated with the abundance of
oak trees in the Bernwood Forest and its surroundings. A cruck is best described
as an A-frame, a pair of massive timbers that run from the ground to the apex of
the roof, usually cut from the same tree. Long Crendon has over 20 cruck houses,
an unusual concentration, but many of the villages round about have a few -
Haddenham has four and Grendon Underwood two, for example. Often hidden
behind render, as here, they are still being discovered.

▼ **Grendon Underwood, Main Road c1965** G230007
Grendon Underwood is a long, straggling village, with the gaps filled steadily from
the 1950s onwards. This view is at the less interesting east end of Main Road, away
from the parish church, the moat, the Georgian rectory and Shakespeare
Farmhouse, where the bard is reputed to have stayed. Attridge's (right) is now
Grendon Stores, and the plot in the foreground now has a 1980s house, a better
design than the dull bungalows on the left of about 1960.

◀ **Waddesdon, Waddesdon
Manor, the South Front 1897**
39653
Now owned by the National
Trust, Waddesdon Manor is a
massive French chateau
deposited on a windswept hilltop
for Baron Ferdinand de
Rothschild, famed for its superb
porcelain collection, fittings
salvaged from French chateaux
and other treasures. Rothschild
used a French architect, the
splendidly-named Hippolyte
Alexandre Gabriel Walter
Destailleur. The work took from
1877 to 1899, and was finished
by Destailleur's son, Andre. This
view is of the wonderfully ornate
and utterly French garden front.

◀ **Waddesdon, Waddesdon Manor, the Aviary 1897** 39663
When Ferdinand Rothschild bought the estate, the hill was virtually devoid of trees; he imported vast numbers of mature trees to create its present wooded character, teams of horses toiling to haul their huge loads up the hill. Rothschild had the grounds landscaped with parterres close to the house, rock mounds, statuary, fountains and this superb aviary, a copy of one from near his childhood home in Germany. It dates from 1889, and combines the aviary with a grotto crammed with Italian statuary.

Waddesdon, The Five Arrows Hotel 1897
39671
Baron Rothschild also greatly improved the village at the foot of the hill. Here, rather than French chateau style, he chose Olde English, a blend of Tudor and Jacobean to rebuild the village hall and the 17th-century almshouses as well as to build numerous houses. Mostly they were designed by Taylor of Bierton in the 1880s. The Five Arrows Hotel is a fine example, dating from 1887; the Gothic-traceried first floor balcony has since been replaced by a Jacobean-style one. The five arrows are the badge of the five Rothschild brothers.

Upper Winchendon, The Wilderness 1897
39666
The Rothschilds also bought the Upper Winchendon and Eythrope estates - indeed, they still live at Eythrope down by the River Thame. The Wilderness, near Upper Winchendon church, is all that remains of a much larger house, more of a palace, built around 1700 by the First Marquess of Wharton and largely demolished by the Duke of Marlborough in 1758. This building, which incorporates 17th-century elements, was the kitchen and service buildings, subsequently altered to form a pretty sizeable mansion in its own right. The creeper has gone, but the house remains little changed.

▲ **Stone, The County Asylum 1897** 39632

Buckinghamshire's County Lunatic Asylum was built at Stone, three miles west of Aylesbury, in the early 1850s. It was given a more ornate entrance building in the 1860s, including the tower. Later renamed rather more tactfully St John's Hospital, it was completely demolished in the 1990s and replaced by housing estates, leaving only the Gothic chapel of 1869, currently boarded up and awaiting a buyer (July 2002). This view looks down Warren Close from the main Aylesbury Road, the chapel on the left just out of view.

▲ **Waddesdon, The Parish Church 1897** 39669

St Michael's parish church is north of the High Street, and a reminder of a pre-Rothschild era for the village, although the chancel was restored at his expense in 1877. Inside, the nave south arcade is partly late 12th-century and of high quality, and so are the rest of the nave arches, which are early 14th-century. The exterior is quite austere, but the interior of the nave makes it worth persevering to find the church key.

Hartwell, The Egyptian Well 1901 47467
This piece of exotica stands on the lane to Lower Hartwell near Aylesbury. Built in 1851 by the then owner of Hartwell House, Dr John Lee, a noted amateur archaeologist, this building with its Egyptian hieroglyphs has now been beautifully restored. The cornice, missing here, has been reinstated complete with its Greek inscription, which translates as 'Water is Best': it is after all a well-head building.

Central Buckingham- shire

North of Aylesbury

Whitchurch, Church Lane c1955 W433008
Church Lane is a short street leading east off the
High Street, which is just behind Frith's
photographer. On the right is the side elevation of
The Priory, now the Priory Hotel, a fine part stone
and part timber-framed house built in the 15th
century. The rear garden with the large trees is now
the hotel car park. Beyond are two houses, the
second one dated 1939. The garage on the left has
been rebuilt further back, but the local friable
Portland limestone walls remain.

Whitchurch, The Parish Church c1955 W433016

Our second tour heads north from Aylesbury to the village of Whitchurch with its long High Street and many fine buildings. Important in the Middle Ages, it had a motte and bailey castle built by Hugh of Bolebec in the early 12th century and a market charter granted in 1245. The parish church is east of the High Street, the castle and market place to the west. The local Portland limestone used by the medieval stonemasons is a crumbly stone and a maintenance nightmare for churchwardens.

Whitchurch, High Street, Northern End c1955 W433005

The next photographs follow the High Street from north to south. Here the photographer looks across the High Street westwards from Church Headland Lane with the start of Market Hill to the left of the thatched cottage, Cobwebs. This now (2002) has a giant spider in thatch crawling across its roof. The timber-framed cottage at the left is of about 1600, but has '1524' cut on a beam.

Whitchurch, High Street, Looking North c1955 W433014
The photographer has moved south and is looking past the early 19th-century White Horse with its painted brick front and the entry to School Lane. Beyond the stone cottages, the nearer now a beauty salon, are the diagonally-set brick flues of the Priory Hotel, a fine 15th- and 16th-century building. The Old House, past the entrance to Church Lane and behind the stone garden wall and high hedge, is also 16th-century.

Whitchurch, High Street c1955 W433010
A little further south, the photographer looks past The Old Cottage, on the west or left side of the High Street, towards the rendered and jettied mid 16th-century Tudor House with the carved bargeboards to its gable end behind the van. Beyond workshops, now a house, the gable with the Gothic window is a Victorian chapel, now a small (closed) fire station. The shop on the right, Fosters, is still the village shop. The garage on the far left still remains, but is no longer an Esso one.

◄ **Whitchurch, High Street, Southern End c1955** W433013
At the south end of the High Street Frith's photographer looks northwards beside the turning on the right into Hawleys Lane. On the corner is The Laurels, a late Victorian bay-windowed villa dated 1897. Behind it is Beech Tree Court, houses formed out of old farmbuildings. On the left the windows facing the camera to the right of the telegraph pole belong to Park House Farm, its brick front concealing a good timber frame; its barns and farm buildings out of view to the left were converted into houses in the 1980s.

◀ Whitchurch, High Street Looking South c1955 W433009

We are looking south to the curve in the High Street. Another jettied timber-framed house, now subdivided, stands to the left. Jettying is the projection of an upper storey beyond a lower one, and in this case the jetty provides a roof for the bay windows. On the other side, behind the approaching lorry is Winster Paddocks with its timber-framed gable facing us. This was the Cock Inn until well into the 20th century, and dates from the mid-16th century.

▼ Whitchurch, The White Swan c1955 W433011

At the south end of the High Street, on the east side, is the 18th-century White Swan, here in its thatched hey-day. The main roofs are now clay tiled, with only the right-hand building still thatched, now altered and incorporated in the pub bar. The pump remains, but the garden at the left is now the pub car park.

◀ Whitchurch, Market Hill c1955 W433003

Market Hill climbs west from the north end of the High Street. Here we look back downhill towards the High Street with the church tower beyond. Hugh de Vere, the lord of the manor and Earl of Oxford, secured a market charter from King Henry III in 1245 and laid out the market place to the north-east and east of the castle, between it and the High Street. It was not as successful as either Aylesbury or Winslow, which are both on the same main road, and by 1400 it had ceased to function.

▼ **Whitchurch, Oving Road, Looking West c1955** W433002

Oving Road leads west uphill from the north end of the High Street - the architectural quality does not fall off. Here the cottages use the three main materials that give Whitchurch its architectural character: timber-framing, local coursed random limestone and brick. The pair of brick cottages are mid 19th-century and an infill between 17th-century cottages, some timber-framed and some stone.

▼ **Oving, The Parish Church and the Black Boy Inn c1955** O118002

Oving, west of Whitchurch, lies off the main road, and is a very pretty village on the Portland limestone ridge. Many people visit the Black Boy Inn, which has expansive views northwards across the vale towards North Marston. The cottage now has its stone exposed, and a lean-to conservatory replaces the brick lean-to. Behind it is the Victorian village school, now a house. Behind the photographer on the left is a good timber-framed thatched cottage.

▲ **Whitchurch, Market Hill c1955** W433001

The castle was to the south of these cottages; its outer bailey was bisected by the later Castle Lane. The market place was encroached upon by later building, and is difficult to identify clearly, but it has several good 17th-century cottages around it, including this range of early 17th-century timber-framed buildings. The distant one is the gable to the one we saw in W433003 (page 51). Market Hill is now a quiet backwater by-passed by the Oving Road to its north.

◀ **Oving, The Butchers Arms c1955** 0118005
Dark Lane leads east from the village street, passing the Butchers Arms, now a house; its original two storeys of chequered brick were given a third storey in the mid 19th century. The cupola beyond belongs to the mid 18th-century former coach house and stable block (now a house in its own right) to 17th-century Oving House, remodelled in the 1740s and enlarged later in the century.

Oving, The Post Office c1955 0118009
This view looks from the North Marston Road along Bowling Alley - a view much changed since the 1950s. The post office and the outbuilding in the foreground have been replaced by 1980s houses. The house with the slate roof by the telegraph pole survives. In the distance the building at right angles to the road is the 1869 Methodist church. The horse-drawn carrier's waggon outside the post office gives a distinctly old fashioned feel to this photograph.

◀ **Steeple Claydon, North End Road c1955** S565020

The Verneys of Claydon House in Middle Claydon, now a National Trust house, bought Steeple Claydon in 1705 from the Chaloner family, who are commemorated in the village road, Chaloners Hill. The village has grown recently thanks to housing estates, but many older buildings survive. This view looks south-west along North End Road past the former pub, now a house. A matching window has been inserted in the middle of the painted Chesham and Brackley Breweries sign, but the rest of the paintwork is still visible. The other cottages also remain, although the far one, No 1, has had the single storey part raised to two storeys.

Quainton, The Parish Church c1955 Q14024

Quainton is nowadays noted for its steam railway collection and tower windmill. Inside the church are superb monuments to the 17th- and 18th-century Dormer family. The medieval church was substantially rebuilt in the 1870s, reusing much of the stone and windows. To the west of the churchyard, just out of this view, are the brick-built Winwood Almshouses of 1687 with their four clusters of four tall brick chimneys.

Steeple Claydon, West Street c1955 S565005

This view looks along West Street, not the most attractive street in the village. The Crown Inn has been converted into a house (2002), and its 1930s steel windows have been replaced by stained timber casements. The three-sided door archway is typical of the Aylesbury Brewery Company's 1930s designs. The railings to the right belong to The Firs, a house of about 1860. On the opposite side of the road, the single-storey building beyond the bay-windowed two-storey house is now a newsagent and a fish and chip shop.

Steeple Claydon, The Parish Church c1955 S565013

Just beyond the far south-east end of the village is the parish church of St Michael. The only medieval spires in the county are at Hanslope and Olney: this one is Victorian, by William Wilkinson of Oxford, added in 1862. It is a landmark for miles around. The nave and chancel are basically medieval, but they are rather spoiled by the high, plain brick transepts: a slightly odd church, and not particularly loveable.

Winslow, Market Square c1960 W432030 In the Middle Ages, Winslow was held by the Abbot of St Albans, who laid out the Market Square and the High Street in the 13th century for his 'new town'. In 1235 a market charter was granted. This view looks across the Market Square; the George (centre left) and the buildings behind are market encroachment from the 16th century onwards. The ornate iron balcony on the George is reputed to have come from Claydon House.

▲ **Winslow, Horn Street c1960** W432045

Horn Street is in the older, western part of the town; the High Street and the Market Square were added to it in the 13th century. The lanes and roads here are far less planned and more higgledy-piggledy. Horn Street is the main street that winds westward; it is full of attractive houses, including The Old Bakery on the right, a 17th-century timber-framed and thatched house. The square tower in the distance is the former Congregational chapel of 1884, now a house.

◀ **Stoke Hammond, The Parish Church c1955**

S566001

This church is one of a number in the Greensand Hills that are built in the distinctive toffee-coloured and misleadingly-named greensand stone. It is an attractive stone usable only for the rubble stone walls; the quoins, windows and doors have to use dressed stone from elsewhere. St Luke's church is cruciform (that is, with a central crossing tower); the tower was inserted into the east end of the nave around 1350, and the transepts were added in the 15th century.

► **Mursley, Main Street c1955** M381012e

Mursley, a couple of miles east of Winslow, is now basically a single main street. Church Lane, which once led to Winslow, is now a dead-end lane. The village is best known for the white-painted concrete water tower on the Whaddon Road, which can be seen for miles around. Here Frith's photographer looks north past the former National School and schoolteacher's house of 1874 to the thatch roof of The Thatch, beyond the pub sign for the Green Man - the pub, a 1930s rebuild, is out of view.

▲ **Mursley, The Parish Church c1955** M381011b

This view of the parish church of St Mary is taken from Main Street, with Church Lane on the left. Like so many medieval churches across central Buckinghamshire, it is built in the crumbly local Portland limestone, and so the church had to be extensively restored in Victorian times. The tower is 15th-century, the rest 14th-century. Behind the photographer is Manor Farm, its 16th-century chimneys rising above an 18th-century brick refronting.

▲ **Stoke Hammond, Main Road and the Post Office c1965** S566012a

The main Leighton Buzzard to Bletchley road winds through the village (the church is on a quiet loop lane), and the post office is on the main road, at the junction with Old Bell Close. This is one of Frith's favourite types of view: the Frith photographers nearly always photographed village post offices, no matter how architecturally unprepossessing, for they were big postcard sellers. This building of about 1910 is still a shop. The telephone kiosk has gone, but the pillar box remains.

Stoke Hammond, The Three Locks c1965 S566012b
South of Stoke Hammond and actually in Soulbury parish are a flight of three locks where the Grand Junction Canal (from 1929 part of the Grand Union Canal) descends 20 feet towards Bletchley. Begun in 1793, the canal from London to Braunston in Northamptonshire was opened in 1805. This view looks north from the Great Brickhill road bridge over the three locks. On the left is the former lock-keeper's cottage, with the Three Locks pub behind. On the right is the small pumping station that brought the water back 'upstream' when required.

Edlesborough, The Bell c1965 E165004

Just off the Chiltern Hills, Edlesborough church with its mid 14th-century west tower can be seen for miles around - it is perched on an isolated chalk hill. Now redundant, it is a fine church with many original medieval features. Edlesborough has a great medieval tithe barn. This view looks along the busy Leighton Road, with the church out of sight to the left and the High Street to the right. All the buildings survive, including the Bell pub.

Edlesborough, The Ford and the Windmill c1965 E165008

South-east of the village, a lane crosses the county boundary with Bedfordshire along the upper reaches of the young River Ouzel. This view is taken from the Bedfordshire bank, with the ford (still in existence) in the foreground. The windmill tower, here derelict, belonged to Edlesborough Mills, which also had a water-wheel powered by the stream. The windmill tower is now restored and part of a house.

Around Buckingham

Buckingham, Market Square c1965 B280083
A disastrous fire in 1725 destroyed about a third of
the town, and many buildings date from after the
fire. The Market Square (actually rectangular)
achieved Georgian grandeur by the end of the
century. As befitted a borough supported by the
Dukes of Buckingham living at nearby Stowe, a new
Town Hall replaced the crumbling 17th-century one
demolished in 1783. The 1784 one (centre)
originally had an open ground floor with assembly
rooms above. The ground floor is now offices, but
the clock tower cupola surmounted by
Buckingham's badge, the chained swan, still
dominates the town.

▼ Buckingham, Bridge Street c1965 B280076

Our third tour starts in Buckingham, once the county town, but rather out on a limb and progressively losing the title to Aylesbury, which was much more centrally situated. The town had an Anglo-Saxon minster church, but it assumed more significance during King Edward the Elder's reconquest of the Danelaw - he built a burh, or fortified town, in the loop of the River Ouse in 917 AD. By the end of the 11th century, the county of Buckinghamshire was in existence. This view looks across the River Ouse towards the Town Hall. The bridge dates from 1805.

▼ Buckingham, The Old Gaol c1955 B280041

In the Middle Ages the county gaol was housed in the castle dungeons, and was often filled with those awaiting trial at the periodic county assizes. However, when the assizes moved to Aylesbury, the town had no gaol, so Lord Cobham of Stowe's campaign to get the assizes back led to him funding a new gaol in 1748. The summer assizes returned until 1848. The gaol stands at the west end of Market Square; it has recently been restored as a museum and tourist information centre.

▲ Buckingham, West Street c1950 B280001

West Street leads to Market Square. It has good Georgian buildings, including the 1720s rendered building on the right, now Jilly Sanders, which in fact re-fronts a most interesting 16th-century house that survived the 1725 fire. The White Hart also survived the fire; it dates from about 1600, and has a most attractive stucco front of about 1840.

◄ **Buckingham, High Street and Cattle Market c1950** B280022
The market place continued east of the Old Gaol into Market Hill and the High Street. The north side of Market Hill has a number of timber-framed buildings, while the market place to the right remains, but without the railings. The lime trees have been replanted since 1950. An ancient borough since at least the 10th century, the town received new charters from Queen Mary in 1554 and then from Charles II in 1684; the names of the bailiffs (mayors from 1684-88) survive from 1312 until 1835. After that date, a new corporation with a mayor came into being.

Buckingham, The Swan and Castle Hotel c1955 B280044
Standing in Castle Street south of the Town Hall, the Swan and Castle has been an inn since at least 1577 - until 1814 it was the White Swan. The early Victorian stuccoed facade has distinctive triple sash windows; the carriage arch to the left leads into a yard lined by inn buildings, outbuilding and stables. The pub is now named the Villiers Hotel, and is thriving again after some parlous years in the 1980s.

Buckingham, Castle Street c1950 B280002
Castle Street once led to the castle on its motte, or mound, which is now occupied by the parish church. The castle existed by the 13th century, but decayed during the late Middle Ages; in the 1670s the motte was levelled by one Henry Robinson to make a bowling green. Robinson also built the best house in Castle Street, Trolly Hall, originally the assembly rooms (left, with the hanging sign outside and the ornate cornice and parapet); it received a Georgian frontage soon after the 1725 fire, and was a solicitors until the 1980s, but is now a house.

Buckingham, The Parish Church from Castle Street c1965 B280089
Further up Castle Street and at its junction with Bristle Hill to the right and Elm Street on the left, the photographer is looking towards the great east window of the parish church. The chancel is the work of the local boy made good, the great Victorian architect Sir George Gilbert Scott, whose father was vicar of nearby Gawcott. The garage with the three-wheeler outside, a good stucco Early Georgian house, is now offices.

Buckingham
The Church of St Peter and St Paul c1955 B280036

The original church had stood south-west of the old castle hill and
opposite the Manor House. The churchyard survives, but the
medieval tower collapsed in 1776. Earl Temple of Stowe gave the
castle hill for a new church (the hilltop had been already levelled in
the 17th century for a bowling green). The church, begun in 1777,
was 18th-century Gothick in style, and the tower and spire remain
relatively intact. However, in the 1860s Sir George Gilbert Scott
transformed the nave inside and out into more 'correct' Gothic,
and added the chancel. The spire was designed as an eye-catcher
from Stowe mansion.

Buckingham, The Manor House, a Twisted Chimney c1955 B280035
Frith's photographer has caught a delightful quirky chimney on the north side of the Manor House in Church Street, a chimney much drawn and photographed by others. The Manor House was originally built as a house for a Lincoln Cathedral prebendary - Buckingham was then in Lincoln diocese. Mostly 16th-century, the north wing is graced by this spiral brick chimney, supported for years by iron stays. On my visit in June 2002 the scene was unchanged since 1955, for the leaded casement window was also wide open.

◀ **Gawcott, Main Street from the West c1960**
G229010
Gawcott, a mile and a half south-west of Buckingham, lies at the head of a stream (flowing north into the River Ouse) whose course runs along the right-hand side of this road. This view looks east along Main Street from beside Leyland Farm. This is not the best end of the village architecturally, but we can see the tower of the parish church of 1827 in the distance.

Buckingham, Chandos Road Board School c1950 B280024
The Board School became Chandos First School, and is now (2002) Grenville Combined School. Its baroque-ish design is unchanged, although the cupola has long gone.

Gawcott, Main Street c1960 G229006
Moving further east along Main Street, we reach the junction with New Inn Lane on the right. Behind the telegraph pole is the small mid 19th-century Methodist chapel with its porch and ornamental bargeboards to the gable. Opposite is a row of cottages; the left-hand one is called Lace Cottage, a reminder of an important cottage industry for women hereabouts, which supplemented the men's meagre agricultural labourers' wages.

Gawcott, Main Street c1960 G229005
Further east, the thatched shop on the left is nowadays a private house, The Old House. Beyond is another thatched cottage, The White House. Behind the wide verge with its young trees is the churchyard of Holy Trinity. The dilapidated church was rebuilt in 1827 to a Georgian design of the then vicar, Thomas Scott. His son, George Gilbert, was born in the vicarage in 1811, and later became one of England's greatest Victorian architects; his work includes the Foreign Office, St Pancras Station Hotel, and the Albert Memorial, all in London.

Gawcott, Main Street c1960 G229014
The best buildings in the village are towards the junction with Radclive Road, and Old Eagles Farmhouse on the left is one of the finest. An 18th-century building in chequered brick, its farmyard is now a close of 1960s houses, Old Barn Close. The house beyond the rendered one on the left, and with an attic window in the gable, is Westcott House, dated 1720 on a stone plaque. The house behind the Morris Traveller, a timber-framed estate car if you like, is Red Lion House, formerly an inn.

▼ Buckingham, Stowe School c1955 B280050

About three miles north-west of Buckingham, Stowe Park is of European importance. Its remarkable 18th-century landscaped park is full of splendid garden temples, sculptures and columns. Now owned by the National Trust (the school had found the park's maintenance an impossible burden), Stowe School is, of course, as famous as the park. It was founded in 1923, rescuing the mansion and park from redevelopment. The mansion's wonderful south front is over four hundred feet wide and has a great central portico - Adam, Vanbrugh and Kent worked on the house.

▼ Buckingham, Stowe Avenue c1955 B280030

The avenue runs a mile and a half from Buckingham to the Corinthian Arch. It was saved from development by Clough Williams-Ellis, the architect of Portmeirion, in the early 1920s, and given to the new Stowe School. The avenue has largely been replanted in a rolling programme of restoration. We can see the Corinthian Arch of 1765-67 in the distance; the road turns left before it reaches it to skirt the grounds and enter them via the Oxford Gate. A whole book could be devoted to Stowe. The grounds are open to the public, and in school holidays so is the house.

◀ Buckingham, The Palladian Bridge, Stowe School c1955 B280069

Originally a small country house, Stowe was developed by the Temples and Grenvilles, later Dukes of Buckingham and Chandos. The great park focuses at the east on the Grecian Valley and the Elysian Fields, while the southern lakes terminate at the Palladian Bridge of 1738, probably by James Gibbs and a perfect essay in the style of Andrea Palladio, the great Venetian architect (he was championed by Inigo Jones in the 17th century and by Lord Burlington in the early 18th century). There are many examples of superb garden architecture like this - the modern visitor marvels at them just as the 18th-century visitor did.

◀ **Maids Moreton, Post Office Corner c1955**

M264001

Maids Moreton is now joined to Buckingham at its south-west end, but it retains its individuality, particularly along Main Street. This view shows Main Street straight ahead and Moreton Road, the A413, turning right towards Buckingham past the front of the thatched cottage. Behind Scott's Farmhouse on the left is a close of 1990s houses, Scotts Farm Close, while there are new houses on the grass opposite, Drakes Corner.

**Maids Moreton
The Post Office c1955**
M264010
The photographer is looking down Main Street from the site of the 1990s houses, Drakes Corner. The old post office is now a dwelling - the post box has been removed; opposite, Harrods was offering a house and eight lots for sale. Later, the site was redeveloped for Walnut Drive, a close of late 1960s houses. Further down Main Street, on the right, was the village blacksmith, commemorated in Forge Cottage; Harris Brothers Engineers kept the business alive into the 21st century.

Maids Moreton, The Village c1955 M264009
This view looks north-west up Main Street, with the gable of Forge Cottage on the left. Pightle Cottage (near right) is a good 17th-century timber-framed and thatched cottage, but the police house (its sign is on the right) is now a private house and extended. The other thatched roof is that of the Wheatsheaf pub, also 17th-century. The village is one of small cottages, many timber-framed with whitewashed infill panels and thatched roofs, and a few larger farmhouses mixed in.

Maids Moreton, The Parish Church c1955 M264007
The parish church is a remarkable one, funded reputedly in the mid 15th century by two wealthy unmarried sisters from Toddington in Bedfordshire - the Peover sisters' generosity is commemorated in the village name of Maids Moreton. Although not large, the church is a superb and complete Perpendicular Gothic building of high quality and some originality, particularly in the west tower's design. It is a church that should be visited, and one of my favourite ones in Buckinghamshire.

Around Stony Stratford

Before the Arrival of Milton Keynes New Town

Stony Stratford
The Parish Church of St Mary and St Giles c1955 S266011

Stony Stratford enjoyed an 18th-century revival as a coaching town; it was the first overnight stop from London on the Roman road named Watling Street. Stony's medieval growth at the bridge over the River Ouse dated from the market charter of 1194. The town suffered a series of disastrous fires in the 18th century; this church was rebuilt after the 1742 fire, but not until the 1770s. The tower is medieval, and the nave was given Gothic windows in the 1870s, while the chancel on the left dates from 1928. The oddly domestic vestry in the foreground was added in 1891.

Stony Stratford, The Church of St Mary Magdalene c1960 S266024
By contrast, further north along the High Street stands an uncompromisingly modern church. This is the Roman Catholic church built in 1957-58 by Deacon and Laing. It is a good example of its period and type, and certainly eschews grandeur. Churches like this can be found everywhere, and one wonders whether they will stand the test of time. There are now metal gates to the left, with the Chi-Rho monogram as a panel in each.

Stony Stratford, Horsefair Green c1965 S266085
The name of this long, narrow and very pretty open space is self-explanatory. Nowadays the green is edged with lime trees; attractive Georgian and later cottages surround it, and the Baptist Chapel of 1823 faces its north side. This view looks north-east past the war memorial cross of about 1920 towards Watling Street, which forms the Green's short east side.

Stony Stratford
The River Great Ouse and the Watermill c1960 S266025

This view looks north-west along the mill cut of the River Ouse towards the watermill off Mill Lane. First mentioned in 1581, it was much rebuilt; what we see here is mostly 19th-century. The building had stopped being a watermill in 1915. After that it was used as engineering and other workshops, but it had declined somewhat before it was destroyed by fire in 1985. The ruins have been demolished, and have been replaced (2002) by an apartment block which vaguely copies the mill buildings. The rest of the site is now covered with houses and flats.

▶ **Calverton, The Village c1955** C495001

A little over a mile south of Stony Stratford and west of Watling Street, the village of Calverton is remarkably unspoilt still. It is divided into three 'wealds' or ends. The church and manor house are at Lower Weald, and this view, taken from the Beachampton road, is virtually unchanged. The irregularities in the field in the foreground are the remnants of the extensive stone pits which yielded the limestone from which Calverton and Stony Stratford were built. The Manor House on the left, a fascinating building, dates from 1500, with 16th- and 17th-century additions.

◄ **Calverton, Manor Cottages c1955** C495002

Stony Stratford's church of St Mary and St Giles (S266011) was a chapel-of-ease to Calverton, while the other church in Stony, St Mary's, belonged to Wolverton. The town only became a parish in its own right after the Restoration of Charles II in 1660. This is a closer view of the cottages we saw in C495001, a row of 18th-century thatched farm labourers' cottages; there were once five, but in 1955 they were merged into three with ugly bathroom extensions at the rear. To the far right is the Old School House of 1857, its modern name giving away its former role.

Wolverton, Stratford Road c1910 W176501
This series of views is actually of what was known as New Wolverton. The village of Old Wolverton lies to its north-west, shrunk away to a few houses and the church, a deserted medieval village. New Wolverton owed its existence to the London and Birmingham Railway, which established its works here in 1838 halfway between the two villages. Initially, and when the London and North Western Railway took over in 1861, steam locomotives were built here, then from about 1865 railway carriages. This view shows the town at its height, with the railway works on the left and the town on the right with the tramway on the Stratford Road between.

◄ **Wolverton, Church Street c1955**

W176022

Parallel to Stratford Road and to the south of it is one of the grid of streets that were laid out for the town from the 1840s, starting at the east and then expanding westward as land was released in the 1850s and 1860s. Further expansion came in the 1890s and in 1904, keeping pace with the expansion of the railway works as the major employer. Most of the buildings on the left survive, although the Victoria Hotel is now Zaks bar and music venue. All on the right was demolished and replaced by a shopping centre and an indoor market, The Agora, in the 1970s.

Wolverton, Stratford Road c1955 W176020
In the 1950s the railway works were still thriving, but from the 1960s they declined, and many of the buildings were demolished. The Wolverton Baths of 1890 survive, and so do several other buildings, including the LNWR Fire Station of 1911, but much of the Stratford Road is now occupied by a Tesco's of 1992, whose facade copies the railway works style. In the far distance the houses have been replaced by the Glyn Square shopping centre of the early 1970s. The tall stuccoed pub on the right is the North Western.

New Bradwell, The Old ▷ Windmill c1955 N224164
New Bradwell is a grid-iron village laid out by the London and North Western Railway in 1852 north of the Grand Junction Canal. Bradwell village is well south of the canal, and was only joined to New Bradwell by the development of the new city of Milton Keynes after 1967. That great new town swallowed up the fields, villages and small towns of central north-east Buckinghamshire after the views in this book were taken; but the old windmill south of the canal survives - indeed, it is being restored. Built in 1816, it ceased working in 1871.

◁ Wolverton, The Grand Union Canal c1960
W176076
The Grand Junction Canal (now the Grand Union) passed east of Old Wolverton; it was crossed by the old turnpike road from Newport Pagnell to Stony Stratford, which is where this view is taken from. We are looking north-west past Old Wolverton Wharf along the canal - a builders' merchant's depot now lies to the left. The canal was begun in 1793. It would have opened in 1803 but for the problem aqueduct over the River Ouse, some 200 metres in the distance. The aqueduct was completed in 1805 but collapsed in 1808; the present iron one, the Iron Trunk Aqueduct, replaced it in 1811. The heavily pruned trees (left) belong to the Galleon, an early 19th-century canal-side pub.

Great Linford, Black Horse Bridge c1965

G347070

Further east along the Grand Junction Canal, the Wolverton Road crosses the canal. The road was formerly on this bridge, but now it is carried on a modern 1960s bridge of less character. Beyond the bridge is another wharf - this one is Stantonbury Wharf, used for loading the sand and gravel extracted from the Great Ouse valley. The Black Horse pub is now the thriving Proud Perch, extended in brick towards the canal.

Woburn Sands, The Woods c1955 W434006
There are a few outcrops of Lower Greensand in central Buckinghamshire, at Brill, for example, but the rocks surface near the Bedfordshire border immediately south of Woburn Sands. The landscape is quite distinctive, with very steep low hills and sandy soils. The Greensand Hills continue east into Bedfordshire; the distinctive deep brown stone (anything but green) is used for buildings and boundary walls. The poor sandy soils were ideal for hunting parks or woodland, and the Buckinghamshire Brickhills are thickly wooded, much of it pine woods mixed with oaks and other deciduous trees, as we see here.

Woburn Sands, The Golf Course c1955 W434024
The wooded heathland lends itself to golf courses: bunker sand is on site in the sandy soil, and the pines and other trees naturalise the course quickly. Perhaps golf courses are the modern successor of the medieval hunting park in making use of poor-quality land. The Woburn Golf and Country Club, south-east of Bow Brickhill and west of Woburn in Bedfordshire, has now developed into a major international golf tournament venue.

Woburn Sands, High Street c1955 W434009
Woburn Sands, right on the Bedfordshire border and bleeding across it, grew up when the railway arrived in 1846; its delightful station in Tudor cottage style is on the Bedford to Bletchley junction line. This view looks along the High Street, with Hardwick Road to the left. The war memorial-cum-clock tower has been relocated away from the more recent roundabouts at the junction to a safer location further up the High Street beside the 1874 Institute. The Swan still thrives, now mostly clad in painted weatherboarding.

◄ **Simpson, Main Road c1958** S570003
Back in the new city of Milton Keynes,
Simpson is one of the villages it
engulfed; but it is conserved within its
boundaries. About two miles north of
Bletchley, with the Grand Union Canal
passing to its west and the River Ouzel
to its right, Simpson has a number of
old cottages and many new city houses
and estates. This view looks south
down the main street towards the
church of St Thomas and St Nicholas -
we can see its 14th-century crossing
tower (centre). On the right is Freedom
Cottage of around 1700, thatched and
with late timber-framing. Beyond are
the hipped roofs of Abbey Road,
former UDC housing of the 1950s.

◀ Woburn Sands, High Street c1955
W434015

Further north along the High Street, the photographer looks past the junction with Vicarage Street past a jumble of piecemeal development, mostly late 19th-century small shops. The post office is still in the right-hand building. The brick wall on the left encloses the grounds of Shelton House, the best building in the village, a late 18th-century brick house predating Woburn Sands' arrival; it is now offices.

▼ Simpson, Main Road c1958
S570002

This view looks north to the thatched cottages, Nos 456 and 458. They were originally built as one farmhouse in the 15th century, and incorporate a cruck frame (we can see the timber-framing of the gable elevation); but the fronts are now in 19th-century brick. Beyond is a thatched barn, now converted into a house, Orchard Barn. The other two houses are now much changed, with extensions and modern windows.

◀ Bow Brickhill, The Parish Church c1960 B451007

Perched on the greensand ridge high above its village, the delightful All Saints' parish church is built in the dark brown stone extracted from the hills around it. In 1960 there were fine views from here across north Buckinghamshire; now trees obscure this completely in summer, but in winter we can look north-west over the new city of Milton Keynes, and at night see its lights spreading as far as the eye can see. The church is mostly 15th-century, with some chalkstone window dressings.

Bletchley, Aylesbury Street c1960 B439057 Bletchley, an old town, expanded greatly in the later 19th century after the railway and mass-production brick making arrived. In the 20th century the town grew greatly before being incorporated into the new city of Milton Keynes in 1967. Aylesbury Street is actually in Fenny Stratford, closer to Watling Street, a village absorbed by Bletchley. In the distance the building with a pitched roof on the left behind the road sign once had two massive 17th-century chimney stacks, each with six great brick diagonal chimney shafts: a great loss.

▼ Bletchley, St Mary's Church c1965 B439126

The old core of Bletchley was around the parish church to the west of the railway, well away from Fenny Stratford, then a separate village with its own parish church by Watling Street. St Mary's church is set in a generous churchyard with a park to the west, which includes the Rectory Cottages Museum in a timber-framed hall house of about 1475. This was built for the de Greys, lords of the manor, one of whom is buried in the church. The church is a grand one, with battlemented parapets and a tall 15th-century west tower.

▼ Bletchley, Bletchley Park, the Entrance Hall c1955 B439042

Inside the mansion, all is sumptuous panelling and enrichment. This view of the entrance hall shows a combination of Jacobean-style panelling with 13th-century-style Gothic arches. The house is now part of the Bletchley Park Trust, who organise guided tours; the various rooms can be hired for conferences and banquets. The house has thus been saved - its future was threatened at one time after the Post Office Training Centre left.

◀ Bletchley, Bletchley Park c1965 B439070

Few people will not have heard of Bletchley Park and its years of glory during World War II. It was here that the German Enigma code was broken; Bletchley Park was a government cryptography and intelligence monitoring centre. The grounds were full of gas- and blast-proof huts, some of which survive - so does the mansion itself. The core is of 1860, but it was expanded and enlarged piecemeal in 1883 and in around 1906 to produce a rather over-busy agglomeration of bay windows, oriels and even a leaded ogee dome.

◄ **Bletchley, Bletchley Park, the Quiet Room c1955** B439041

At the time of the photograph, this was the Quiet Room for the Post Office National Training Centre. Originally, it was the mansion's library, which was installed in the 1880s. It was a curiously oppressive room - the elaborate Jacobethan-style plaster ceiling is more suited to a room with a 20ft-high ceiling than an 8ft one. It is now again called the library, and is used as a seminar and meeting room by the Bletchley Park Trust. The mansion has a Churchill Memorabilia Collection and a Toy Museum; various buildings in the grounds house the 'Enigma @ Bletchley Park' exhibition, and the visitor can follow a Cryptology Trail.

Bletchley, Church Green Road c1955 B439018
To the west of the church, Church Green Road leads westward, once with a number of old thatched cottages. This view is a sad one today, for both thatched cottages have been demolished. The left-hand one, built in the early 17th century, was replaced by a 1960s bungalow. The right-hand one, also 17th-century and with a picturesque sweep of thatched roofs, was demolished for road improvement. Note the old school warning sign of a burning torch.

Bletchley, Central Gardens c1955 B439022
Just as in B439018, much has changed in this view. Central Park ran from Queensway to the back of Western Road, whose c1900 houses can be seen in the distance. In the 1950s it was a typical town centre park with seats, walks and flower beds, but all this changed when the Leisure Centre arrived in 1971-76, with its pyramidal pool building and large sports hall. This area is now the car park and grass margin to the rear service access road.

Newport Pagnell
and the Far North of Bucks

Newport Pagnell
High Street looking West c1955 N62032

Newport Pagnell, nowadays mostly known as the home of Aston Martin cars (whose factories occupy the site of the long-defunct Salmon's stage coach works), is an ancient town. Strategically situated where the rivers Great Ouse and Ouzel meet, 'Newport' was no longer new by the Norman Conquest: it is one of the oldest two boroughs in the county - the other is Buckingham. A river bridge was recorded in 1187, and a market charter was granted by Gervase de Paganell to the monks of Tickford Priory in 1187. Indeed, some time around then de Paganell's name was added to the town's name.

◁ **Newport Pagnell, Ousebank Gardens 1956** N62031
The High Street turns north, and it and the town end abruptly at the River Great Ouse, which flows through meadows liable to flooding. The ground drops to the river, which is crossed by a bridge on the Northampton Road. This view is in the grounds, now a public park, of Ousebank House, a fine late 17th-century brick house with giant pilasters. It is now occupied by the British Legion. The sandpit has been filled in, and the opposite bank of the Great Ouse is more overgrown.

◄ **Newport Pagnell, The Swan Hotel 1956**
N62043

The best group of older buildings is still at the east end of the High Street. The grandest is the Swan Revived Hotel, whose towering three-storey stuccoed front of about 1840 conceals a 17th-century inn. The parish church is just south of the High Street - we can see its tower (centre left). At the far left, closing the vista where the street bends, is Odell, with a superb columned early 19th-century shopfront. This was an ironmonger's for many years, but it is now a restaurant that perpetuates the shop-keeping family's name.

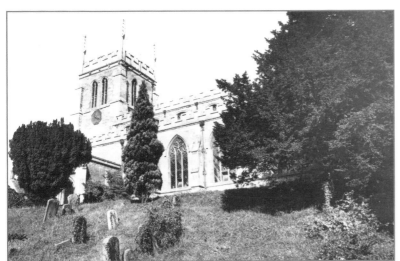

◄ **Newport Pagnell, The Parish Church c1965** N62068

From this view it is obvious that the town occupies a ridge between the two rivers: the land drops to the Great Ouse (see the previous views) and to the Ouzel, as we see here - this view was taken from well down the slope towards its banks. The church is a proud, large town church of high architectural quality. Mostly 14th- and 15th-century, it was completed by the addition of the great west tower between 1542 and 1548.

▼ **Newport Pagnell, High Street looking East c1955** N62022
Back on the High Street, Frith's photographer looks east past the junction with St John Street on the right. The two buildings on this corner were demolished for road improvement and replaced by two cheap and nasty two-storey flat-roofed shops in 1966. On the left all survives as far as and including the Gothic Barclays Bank of 1870. Beyond, all was demolished for road widening in the 1970s. The bow-fronted building straight ahead is Odell, in the 1950s an ironmongers, now a restaurant.

▼ **Newport Pagnell, High Street looking East 1967** N62071
Further west, the High Street widens by the Dolphin pub (left). The building next to it with the plough on its roof, Cooper's the butchers in the 1950s, was replaced in the 1990s by a two-storey bank. The hipped-roofed house two windows wide and three storey high beyond is now the offices of Newport Pagnell Town Council. In the far distance is Odell the ironmonger, a crucial building in the street scene.

▲ **Newport Pagnell, North Bridge from the Play Pen 1956** N62050
The photographer has now moved down to the steps by the river, which still survive. The bridge dates from about 1810 - it replaced earlier ones. It was originally paid for by tolls, and there is a former toll house at its north end. The children are obviously enjoying fishing and swimming. The pointed arch beyond the shirt-sleeved child is a remnant of the medieval river bridge.

◄ **Newport Pagnell, High Street looking West 1956**

N62044

Looking the other way past the Dolphin, the first building is Brewery House, a good early 18th-century brick house, restored in the 1970s. Beyond are the former brewery buildings with later garage doors in the ground floor. These have been swept away and replaced by an overscaled two- and three-storey 1990s brick building with a clutter of hipped tiled roofs, housing a medical centre and Boots.

◄ Newport Pagnell, Tickford Abbey c1965 N62064

This slightly severe-looking three-storey mansion was built in 1767 on the site of a Benedictine priory, long ruinous and partly converted to a house around 1550. The house was given more Gothic trim in the early 19th century, and is now a residential home for the elderly. The Priory was founded by Fulk Peynel (or Pagnell) in the early 12th century. The foundations of the church have been discovered over the years, and a few carved stones and fragments have been incorporated into the house. It overlooks the River Ouzel to the north, but there are housing estates to its south.

◀ **Newport Pagnell, Tickford Bridge 1962** N62062
Back down St John Street, the road descends to cross the River Ouzel on this elegant cast iron bridge dated 1810. It was designed by Henry Provis of Paddington, copying in scaled-down form a larger bridge at Sunderland. It is claimed locally to be the oldest cast iron bridge in England still carrying heavy traffic.

▼ **Newport Pagnell, Wolverton Road c1955** N62036
West from the High Street, Wolverton Road was developed piecemeal; this view looking towards the Manor Road turning makes this abundantly clear. There are Edwardian terraced houses on the left with their distinctive bay windows, on the right are 1920s and 1930s houses, while beyond on the other side of the Manor Road turn are terraces of 1880s artisan houses.

◀ **Newport Pagnell, Queens Avenue c1955**
N62042
Queens Avenue is part of a small 1950s council estate built off the High Street to the north-west of the former brewery. The houses are almost new in this view; the matured gardens have softened the streetscape since, and the good, solid and well-proportioned pairs of semi-detached houses are well looked after.

Newport Pagnell, The M1 Motorway c1965 N62057
England's motorways were enough of a novelty in the early 1960s for Frith's photographers to record them for picture postcard purposes. This now almost surreal view of a near-empty M1 (far from the case in July 2002!) looks north-east from the Little Linford Lane road bridge over the motorway. The Buckinghamshire section of the M1 opened in 1959 on its way from London towards Birmingham.

Newport Pagnell, Newport Pagnell Services, the M1 Motorway c1965 N62058
That much-maligned but vital facility of the motorway network, the service station, was an early landmark. Newport Pagnell Services is now (2002) run by Welcome Break, but it is architecturally very little changed, with the glazed bridge a distinctive feature. This view looks south-east from the same Little Linford Lane bridge. Note the pipework in the central reservation protected by a few irregularly placed cones: a far cry from today's safety-conscious contra-flows and dense forests of cones.

Sherington, The Knoll c1960 S567018
Two miles north-east of Newport Pagnell beyond a loop of the River Great Ouse, Sherington village has three 'ends' or clusters of houses linked by lanes, with a scattering of older cottages and farms. The Stony Stratford to Bedford road, turnpiked in the 18th century, passes to the south, while the 1980s Newport Pagnell by-pass has taken the north-south through traffic out of the village. This view looks from the village green, The Knoll, along Church Road. The bus shelter is now in stone. On the far right is a lorry outside the engineering works of C J Haynes & Son, still in business today.

Sherington, Church Road c1965 S567011
Further up Church Road, we are looking at the backs of 18th-century houses on Church End, the lane which leads to the medieval parish church of St Laud, out of shot to the left. The church has a tall central tower, partly 13th-century, with the upper stages 15th-century. On the left are 1950s bungalows and a chalet bungalow: unfortunately, the village has much infill of this sort of 'anywheresville' stuff. More modern infill is much better, and mostly in the more appropriate stone.

◀ **Lavendon, St Michael's Church, the Interior c1965** L201026
Inside, the evidence for Anglo-Saxon work is mostly at a higher level: the late 12th-century arches were inserted when the aisles were added, and the chancel arch was enlarged at the same time. Only Wing, north of Aylesbury, has as much Anglo-Saxon fabric as Lavendon in the whole of Buckinghamshire. The pulpit is Jacobean, but the pews and chancel fittings are Victorian.

Sherington, Crofts End c1960

S567004

We are looking south-west down Crofts End, the lane which leads from Crofts End itself at the top of the hill behind the photographer to the main through road. The car is parked outside the former Congregational chapel, dated 1822, and converted to housing. Beyond are the well-treed grounds of Manor Farm, where a large moat used to contain the manor house; this was demolished in 1770 and rebuilt outside the moat and fronting the main road.

Lavendon, The Parish Church c1965

L201020

The busy A428 Northampton to Bedford Road winds through the village from west to east, curving round the parish churchyard's rubblestone retaining walls. This is the furthest north part of Buckinghamshire, beyond the stone-built market town of Olney, and not far from the Northamptonshire border. West of the village, in the quiet valley of a stream, was a small abbey founded in 1154, and long-vanished. Lavendon's parish church was old even then, for its nave, part of the chancel and the west tower below the belfry are all late Anglo-Saxon, probably early 11th century.

Lavendon, The Post Offie c1965 L201024

Looking across from within the churchyard is the post office, which occupies an 18th-century stone house. The steel windows replaced the original leaded casements in about 1960, and have themselves been replaced by timber windows ten years ago. That was when the building ceased to be a post office and became a private house. The post office moved into the building to the right with the striped awning.

▼ **Hanslope, The Green c1960** H374008

Leaving the east corner of the churchyard, which itself is at the south-west corner of the village, we reach The Green, its tree now gone. Across Park Road on the other side of The Green is the side gable of Malting Farmhouse, which is dated 1624.

▶ **Hanslope, The Parish Church c1955** H374009

Our last visit in this book is to Hanslope, a stone village north-west of Newport Pagnell and one that feels more like Northamptonshire than Buckinghamshire. St James's church is one of two churches in the county with a medieval spire (Olney is the other): all the others are Victorian or later. It was built in 1414 and was originally over 200 feet high, but was rebuilt 20 feet lower after being struck by lightning in 1804. The church also has a late Norman chancel.

▲ **Lavendon, The Square and High Street c1965**
L201019

This view is further south-east, looking along the High Street from the junction with Olney Road behind the photographer. In front is the war memorial in the form of a Celtic cross. On the left is the former Lavendon Free School of 1839; it is now houses, with the modern school behind. On the right is the 1895 Union Chapel, now Lavendon Baptist Church. Beyond is the Horseshoe pub.

◄ **Lavendon, The Horseshoe and the Village Hall c1965**

L201016

This view is taken from the grounds of Lavendon Combined School, a modern building that replaced the original one of 1839 which we can see in L201019. The Horseshoe pub has 17th-century origins, and its outbuildings survive intact. To the right is the Village Hall: not great architecture, and made even less so now by a 1970s flat-roofed front extension.

Hanslope, The Square c1955 H374005
North of The Green and Church Lane is Market Square - the High Street runs north from it. This was part of a small planned market town, its market long defunct. This view looks east towards Gold Street, which runs parallel to the High Street. The building on the right is Green Manor, a colourwashed and rendered 17th-century stone building; until the early 1950s it was the Green Man Inn. The thatched cottages on the left, Horseshoe Cottages, have 18th-century stonework concealing a medieval cruck-framed house.

Hanslope, High Street looking South c1955 H374003
The last view in the book looks south-east along the High Street past the long terrace of 1850s cottages on the left. Market Square is in the far distance. The church spire appears to be behind the houses on the right, but in fact it is well south of them. The Shell garage on the right has given way to a close of 1980s houses. Beyond are several good 18th- and early 19th-century houses.

Index

Frith Book Co Titles

www.francisfrith.co.uk

The Frith Book Company publishes over 100 new titles each year. A selection of those currently available are listed below. For latest catalogue please contact Frith Book Co.

Town Books 96 pages, approx 100 photos. County and Themed Books 128 pages, approx 150 photos (unless specified). All titles hardback laminated case and jacket except those indicated pb (paperback)

Amersham, Chesham & Rickmansworth (pb)		
	1-85937-340-2	£9.99
Ancient Monuments & Stone Circles	1-85937-143-4	£17.99
Aylesbury (pb)	1-85937-227-9	£9.99
Bakewell	1-85937-113-2	£12.99
Barnstaple (pb)	1-85937-300-3	£9.99
Bath (pb)	1-85937419-0	£9.99
Bedford (pb)	1-85937-205-8	£9.99
Berkshire (pb)	1-85937-191-4	£9.99
Berkshire Churches	1-85937-170-1	£17.99
Blackpool (pb)	1-85937-382-8	£9.99
Bognor Regis (pb)	1-85937-431-x	£9.99
Bournemouth	1-85937-067-5	£12.99
Bradford (pb)	1-85937-204-x	£9.99
Brighton & Hove(pb)	1-85937-192-2	£8.99
Bristol (pb)	1-85937-264-3	£9.99
British Life A Century Ago (pb)	1-85937-213-9	£9.99
Buckinghamshire (pb)	1-85937-200-7	£9.99
Camberley (pb)	1-85937-222-8	£9.99
Cambridge (pb)	1-85937-422-0	£9.99
Cambridgeshire (pb)	1-85937-420-4	£9.99
Canals & Waterways (pb)	1-85937-291-0	£9.99
Canterbury Cathedral (pb)	1-85937-179-5	£9.99
Cardiff (pb)	1-85937-093-4	£9.99
Carmarthenshire	1-85937-216-3	£14.99
Chelmsford (pb)	1-85937-310-0	£9.99
Cheltenham (pb)	1-85937-095-0	£9.99
Cheshire (pb)	1-85937-271-6	£9.99
Chester	1-85937-090-x	£12.99
Chesterfield	1-85937-378-x	£9.99
Chichester (pb)	1-85937-228-7	£9.99
Colchester (pb)	1-85937-188-4	£8.99
Cornish Coast	1-85937-163-9	£14.99
Cornwall (pb)	1-85937-229-5	£9.99
Cornwall Living Memories	1-85937-248-1	£14.99
Cotswolds (pb)	1-85937-230-9	£9.99
Cotswolds Living Memories	1-85937-255-4	£14.99
County Durham	1-85937-123-x	£14.99
Croydon Living Memories	1-85937-162-0	£9.99
Cumbria	1-85937-101-9	£14.99
Dartmoor	1-85937-145-0	£14.99
Derby (pb)	1-85937-367-4	£9.99
Derbyshire (pb)	1-85937-196-5	£9.99
Devon (pb)	1-85937-297-x	£9.99
Dorset (pb)	1-85937-269-4	£9.99
Dorset Churches	1-85937-172-8	£17.99
Dorset Coast (pb)	1-85937-299-6	£9.99
Dorset Living Memories	1-85937-210-4	£14.99
Down the Severn	1-85937-118-3	£14.99
Down the Thames (pb)	1-85937-278-3	£9.99
Down the Trent	1-85937-311-9	£14.99
Dublin (pb)	1-85937-231-7	£9.99
East Anglia (pb)	1-85937-265-1	£9.99
East London	1-85937-080-2	£14.99
East Sussex	1-85937-130-2	£14.99
Eastbourne	1-85937-061-6	£12.99
Edinburgh (pb)	1-85937-193-0	£8.99
England in the 1880s	1-85937-331-3	£17.99
English Castles (pb)	1-85937-434-4	£9.99
English Country Houses	1-85937-161-2	£17.99
Essex (pb)	1-85937-270-8	£9.99
Exeter	1-85937-126-4	£12.99
Exmoor	1-85937-132-9	£14.99
Falmouth	1-85937-066-7	£12.99
Folkestone (pb)	1-85937-124-8	£9.99
Glasgow (pb)	1-85937-190-6	£9.99
Gloucestershire	1-85937-102-7	£14.99
Great Yarmouth (pb)	1-85937-426-3	£9.99
Greater Manchester (pb)	1-85937-266-x	£9.99
Guildford (pb)	1-85937-410-7	£9.99
Hampshire (pb)	1-85937-279-1	£9.99
Hampshire Churches (pb)	1-85937-207-4	£9.99
Harrogate	1-85937-423-9	£9.99
Hastings & Bexhill (pb)	1-85937-131-0	£9.99
Heart of Lancashire (pb)	1-85937-197-3	£9.99
Helston (pb)	1-85937-214-7	£9.99
Hereford (pb)	1-85937-175-2	£9.99
Herefordshire	1-85937-174-4	£14.99
Hertfordshire (pb)	1-85937-247-3	£9.99
Horsham (pb)	1-85937-432-8	£9.99
Humberside	1-85937-215-5	£14.99
Hythe, Romney Marsh & Ashford	1-85937-256-2	£9.99

Available from your local bookshop or from the publisher

Frith Book Co Titles (continued)

Title	ISBN	Price	Title	ISBN	Price
Ipswich (pb)	1-85937-424-7	£9.99	St Ives (pb)	1-85937415-8	£9.99
Ireland (pb)	1-85937-181-7	£9.99	Scotland (pb)	1-85937-182-5	£9.99
Isle of Man (pb)	1-85937-268-6	£9.99	Scottish Castles (pb)	1-85937-323-2	£9.99
Isles of Scilly	1-85937-136-1	£14.99	Sevenoaks & Tunbridge	1-85937-057-8	£12.99
Isle of Wight (pb)	1-85937-429-8	£9.99	Sheffield, South Yorks (pb)	1-85937-267-8	£9.99
Isle of Wight Living Memories	1-85937-304-6	£14.99	Shrewsbury (pb)	1-85937-325-9	£9.99
Kent (pb)	1-85937-189-2	£9.99	Shropshire (pb)	1-85937-326-7	£9.99
Kent Living Memories	1-85937-125-6	£14.99	Somerset	1-85937-153-1	£14.99
Lake District (pb)	1-85937-275-9	£9.99	South Devon Coast	1-85937-107-8	£14.99
Lancaster, Morecambe & Heysham (pb)	1-85937-233-3	£9.99	South Devon Living Memories	1-85937-168-x	£14.99
Leeds (pb)	1-85937-202-3	£9.99	South Hams	1-85937-220-1	£14.99
Leicester	1-85937-073-x	£12.99	Southampton (pb)	1-85937-427-1	£9.99
Leicestershire (pb)	1-85937-185-x	£9.99	Southport (pb)	1-85937-425-5	£9.99
Lincolnshire (pb)	1-85937-433-6	£9.99	Staffordshire	1-85937-047-0	£12.99
Liverpool & Merseyside (pb)	1-85937-234-1	£9.99	Stratford upon Avon	1-85937-098-5	£12.99
London (pb)	1-85937-183-3	£9.99	Suffolk (pb)	1-85937-221-x	£9.99
Ludlow (pb)	1-85937-176-0	£9.99	Suffolk Coast	1-85937-259-7	£14.99
Luton (pb)	1-85937-235-x	£9.99	Surrey (pb)	1-85937-240-6	£9.99
Maidstone	1-85937-056-x	£14.99	Sussex (pb)	1-85937-184-1	£9.99
Manchester (pb)	1-85937-198-1	£9.99	Swansea (pb)	1-85937-167-1	£9.99
Middlesex	1-85937-158-2	£14.99	Tees Valley & Cleveland	1-85937-211-2	£14.99
New Forest	1-85937-128-0	£14.99	Thanet (pb)	1-85937-116-7	£9.99
Newark (pb)	1-85937-366-6	£9.99	Tiverton (pb)	1-85937-178-7	£9.99
Newport, Wales (pb)	1-85937-258-9	£9.99	Torbay	1-85937-063-2	£12.99
Newquay (pb)	1-85937-421-2	£9.99	Truro	1-85937-147-7	£12.99
Norfolk (pb)	1-85937-195-7	£9.99	Victorian and Edwardian Cornwall	1-85937-252-x	£14.99
Norfolk Living Memories	1-85937-217-1	£14.99	Victorian & Edwardian Devon	1-85937-253-8	£14.99
Northamptonshire	1-85937-150-7	£14.99	Victorian & Edwardian Kent	1-85937-149-3	£14.99
Northumberland Tyne & Wear (pb)	1-85937-281-3	£9.99	Vic & Ed Maritime Album	1-85937-144-2	£17.99
North Devon Coast	1-85937-146-9	£14.99	Victorian and Edwardian Sussex	1-85937-157-4	£14.99
North Devon Living Memories	1-85937-261-9	£14.99	Victorian & Edwardian Yorkshire	1-85937-154-x	£14.99
North London	1-85937-206-6	£14.99	Victorian Seaside	1-85937-159-0	£17.99
North Wales (pb)	1-85937-298-8	£9.99	Villages of Devon (pb)	1-85937-293-7	£9.99
North Yorkshire (pb)	1-85937-236-8	£9.99	Villages of Kent (pb)	1-85937-294-5	£9.99
Norwich (pb)	1-85937-194-9	£8.99	Villages of Sussex (pb)	1-85937-295-3	£9.99
Nottingham (pb)	1-85937-324-0	£9.99	Warwickshire (pb)	1-85937-203-1	£9.99
Nottinghamshire (pb)	1-85937-187-6	£9.99	Welsh Castles (pb)	1-85937-322-4	£9.99
Oxford (pb)	1-85937-411-5	£9.99	West Midlands (pb)	1-85937-289-9	£9.99
Oxfordshire (pb)	1-85937-430-1	£9.99	West Sussex	1-85937-148-5	£14.99
Peak District (pb)	1-85937-280-5	£9.99	West Yorkshire (pb)	1-85937-201-5	£9.99
Penzance	1-85937-069-1	£12.99	Weymouth (pb)	1-85937-209-0	£9.99
Peterborough (pb)	1-85937-219-8	£9.99	Wiltshire (pb)	1-85937-277-5	£9.99
Piers	1-85937-237-6	£17.99	Wiltshire Churches (pb)	1-85937-171-x	£9.99
Plymouth	1-85937-119-1	£12.99	Wiltshire Living Memories	1-85937-245-7	£14.99
Poole & Sandbanks (pb)	1-85937-251-1	£9.99	Winchester (pb)	1-85937-428-x	£9.99
Preston (pb)	1-85937-212-0	£9.99	Windmills & Watermills	1-85937-242-2	£17.99
Reading (pb)	1-85937-238-4	£9.99	Worcester (pb)	1-85937-165-5	£9.99
Romford (pb)	1-85937-319-4	£9.99	Worcestershire	1-85937-152-3	£14.99
Salisbury (pb)	1-85937-239-2	£9.99	York (pb)	1-85937-199-x	£9.99
Scarborough (pb)	1-85937-379-8	£9.99	Yorkshire (pb)	1-85937-186-8	£9.99
St Albans (pb)	1-85937-341-0	£9.99	Yorkshire Living Memories	1-85937-166-3	£14.99

See Frith books on the internet www.francisfrith.co.uk

FRITH PRODUCTS & SERVICES

Francis Frith would doubtless be pleased to know that the pioneering publishing venture he started in 1860 still continues today. A hundred and forty years later, The Francis Frith Collection continues in the same innovative tradition and is now one of the foremost publishers of vintage photographs in the world. Some of the current activities include:

Interior Decoration

Today Frith's photographs can be seen framed and as giant wall murals in thousands of pubs, restaurants, hotels, banks, retail stores and other public buildings throughout the country. In every case they enhance the unique local atmosphere of the places they depict and provide reminders of gentler days in an increasingly busy and frenetic world.

Product Promotions

Frith products are used by many major companies to promote the sales of their own products or to reinforce their own history and heritage. Frith promotions have been used by Hovis bread, Courage beers, Scots Porage Oats, Colman's mustard, Cadbury's foods, Mellow Birds coffee, Dunhill pipe tobacco, Guinness, and Bulmer's Cider.

Genealogy and Family History

As the interest in family history and roots grows world-wide, more and more people are turning to Frith's photographs of Great Britain for images of the towns, villages and streets where their ancestors lived; and, of course, photographs of the churches and chapels where their ancestors were christened, married and buried are an essential part of every genealogy tree and family album.

Frith Products

All Frith photographs are available Framed or just as Mounted Prints and Posters (size 23 x 16 inches). These may be ordered from the address below. From time to time other products - Address Books, Calendars, Table Mats, etc - are available.

The Internet

Already twenty thousand Frith photographs can be viewed and purchased on the internet through the Frith websites and a myriad of partner sites.

For more detailed information on Frith companies and products, look at these sites:

www.francisfrith.co.uk
www.francisfrith.com
(for North American visitors)

See the complete list of Frith Books at:

www.francisfrith.co.uk

This web site is regularly updated with the latest list of publications from the Frith Book Company. If you wish to buy books relating to another part of the country that your local bookshop does not stock, you may purchase on-line.

For further information, trade, or author enquiries please contact us at the address below:
The Francis Frith Collection, Frith's Barn, Teffont, Salisbury, Wiltshire, England SP3 5QP.
Tel: +44 (0)1722 716 376 Fax: +44 (0)1722 716 881 Email: sales@francisfrith.co.uk

See Frith books on the internet www.francisfrith.co.uk

TO RECEIVE YOUR FREE MOUNTED PRINT

Mounted Print
Overall size 14 x 11 inches

Cut out this Voucher and return it with your remittance for £2.25 to cover postage and handling, to UK addresses. For overseas addresses please include £4.00 post and handling. Choose any photograph included in this book. Your SEPIA print will be A4 in size, and mounted in a cream mount with burgundy rule line, overall size 14 x 11 inches.

Order additional Mounted Prints at HALF PRICE (only £7.49 each*)

If there are further pictures you would like to order, possibly as gifts for friends and family, purchase them at half price (no additional postage and handling required).

Have your Mounted Prints framed*

For an additional £14.95 per print you can have your chosen Mounted Print framed in an elegant polished wood and gilt moulding, overall size 16 x 13 inches (no additional postage and handling required).

---

* IMPORTANT!
These special prices are only available if ordered using the original voucher on this page (no copies permitted) and at the same time as your free Mounted Print, for delivery to the same address

---

Frith Collectors' Guild

From time to time we publish a magazine of news and stories about Frith photographs and further special offers of Frith products. If you would like 12 months FREE membership, please return this form.

Send completed forms to:
The Francis Frith Collection, Frith's Barn, Teffont, Salisbury, Wiltshire SP3 5QP

Voucher for **FREE** and Reduced Price Frith Prints

Picture no.	Page number	Qty	Mounted @ £7.49	Framed + £14.95	Total Cost
		1	**Free of charge***	£	£
			£7.49	£	£
			£7.49	£	£
			£7.49	£	£
			£7.49	£	£
			£7.49	£	£

Please allow 28 days for delivery	*** Post & handling**	£2.25
Book Title	**Total Order Cost**	£

Please do not photocopy this voucher. Only the original is valid, so please cut it out and return it to us.

I enclose a cheque / postal order for £ . . . .
made payable to 'The Francis Frith Collection'
OR please debit my Mastercard / Visa / Switch / Amex card
(credit cards please on all overseas orders)

Number . . . .

Issue No (Switch only) . . . . .Valid from (Amex/Switch) . . . .

Expires . . . . Signature . . . .

Name Mr/Mrs/Ms . . . .

Address . . . .

. . . .

Postcode . . . . Daytime Tel No . . . .

Email Address . . . .

Valid to 31/12/04

The Francis Frith Collectors' Guild

Please enrol me as a member for 12 months free of charge.

Name Mr/Mrs/Ms . . . .

Address . . . .

. . . .

. . . . Postcode . . . .

Would you like to find out more about Francis Frith?

We have recently recruited some entertaining speakers who are happy to visit local groups, clubs and societies to give an illustrated talk documenting Frith's travels and photographs. If you are a member of such a group and are interested in hosting a presentation, we would love to hear from you.

Our speakers bring with them a small selection of our local town and county books, together with sample prints. They are happy to take orders. A small proportion of the order value is donated to the group who have hosted the presentation. The talks are therefore an excellent way of fundraising for small groups and societies.

Can you help us with information about any of the Frith photographs in this book?

We are gradually compiling an historical record for each of the photographs in the Frith archive. It is always fascinating to find out the names of the people shown in the pictures, as well as insights into the shops, buildings and other features depicted.

If you recognize anyone in the photographs in this book, or if you have information not already included in the author's caption, do let us know. We would love to hear from you, and will try to publish it in future books or articles.

Our production team

Frith books are produced by a small dedicated team at offices in the converted Grade II listed 18th-century barn at Teffont near Salisbury, illustrated above. Most have worked with the Frith Collection for many years. All have in common one quality: they have a passion for the Frith Collection. The team is constantly expanding, but currently includes:

Jason Buck, John Buck, Douglas Burns, Ruth Butler, Angie Chick, Heather Crisp, Isobel Hall, Hazel Heaton, Peter Horne, James Kinnear, Tina Leary, Hannah Marsh, Sue Molloy, Kate Rotondetto, Dean Scource, Eliza Sackett, Terence Sackett, Sandra Sanger, Lewis Taylor, Shelley Tolcher, Clive Wathen and Jenny Wathen.